The Power of Softness
Emotional, Conversational, and Physical Strength Using Inner Martial Arts

How is being emotionally soft a strength? I can only tell you about my experiences when it comes to softness, but I'm not the first person to understand this principle in martial arts. Applying softness as a strength, however, to everyday life, including movements, emotions, and conversations, might be a new twist on an ancient concept.

Tai Chi means, "supreme ultimate." A combination of two forces, yin and yang, which are opposing, yet united forces that dance and evolve into each other. Tai Chi's soft movements and breathing practices are respected around the world.

Wing Chun's focus is to relax and unwind tension. It is also known as "beautiful springtime." It is deceptively strong and sneaky. It can be mastered by men and women of all ages, abilities, and sizes, because it relies on something more subtle than blunt, brute strength.

Jujitsu means, "the gentle art." "Ju," in this case, denotes giving way. The word Aikido translates roughly as the way of energy in harmony. The underlying concept behind both Judo and Aikido is to *go with* opposing forces and use them rather than resist them. Allow them in, and make use of them. While that may be gentle, it can also be deadly.

All of these powerful martial arts have one thing in common, and that is an element of softness. Softness is strength.

Even in Krav Maga, not known for softness, the rule still is, *hard on soft and soft on hard.* If your hard knuckles are heading for a soft nose and the person moves, presenting a jaw or forehead, you could break your hand. Instead, you use your lower palm near the wrist and switch to a *soft palm strike.*

This same rule is true in relationships and conversations. If someone hardens up, the best way to respond is not to harden back. Though it's counterintuitive, you switch to a softer stance. This is protective, and this is strength. It is authentic, powerful strength.

Learning softness as strength was quite a discovery. This revelation came to me by serendipitous surprise when I stumbled upon an unremarkable dojo over 25 years ago.

This dojo practiced a form of Aikido that turned out to be a powerful life tool. They focused almost entirely on the use of Ki. Ki, which is the Japanese word for Chi, as in Tai Chi, is the life force that runs through everything.

In this dojo, they taught that you can increase your Ki using specific practices, and that Ki would leak out into your daily life, eventually. My hope, however, is that you use the practices in this book to infuse Ki into everyday life, as a way of life, as you live, move, and breathe. If you do that, you won't have to pursue finding an unusual dojo.

Incorporate Ki intentionally, with purpose and with your full attention. You pour Ki energy into every magnificent and boring thing you do throughout your life. using normal life as a practice; as your dojo.

I am a mother of four boys all less than two years apart. Getting into my life when I was overwhelmed was a challenge, and I needed this Ki practice as a way to stop fighting my reality; a way to enjoy my busy family life.

Erickson is my son, was my business partner, and now he is my literal ghost writer. When he died unexpectedly from a heart tumor, I would have spiraled downward quickly, were it not for this practice. The road is long for all of us, but I am grateful to have a way to move through life with grace. I hope I can pass along some of these practices that comfort and strengthen you in difficult times, and enhance the adventure of living.

I first learned about Ki 25 years ago in a small, unusual dojo. The reality of this ethereal Ki, its inner power and light, takes your breath away. It was different than anything I had ever practiced or heard about. When I asked one of the students at this new dojo more about Ki, this young orange belt offered her thoughts. "It is difficult to explain. It's doing every movement and technique as if it were a meditation, and then others feel your movement more intensely. You can practice putting Ki into movement and increase its power. Almost right away, you'll get results, and those results will continue to grow." I thought it was an interesting idea, but it wasn't something I believed in at the time.

A man came out from a door in a little office. I hadn't met him before, but the room fell silent and somber once he appeared. When he bowed deeply and entered onto the mat, there was a feeling. I didn't know how to process it, but it was thick and palpable.

The culture in this dojo included preferential treatment and a worship-like respect for teachers and higher ranks. This rubbed me the wrong way. Growing up, I was taught that we were all equals, and no one deserves better treatment because of their status in life. Of course, I still believe this is true, but I also honor the work that one does to increase inner power and presence.

The power of soft presence draws you in, and makes you want to bring that person closer. Strangely, you learn Ki just by being in their vicinity. When you practice this Ki in everyday life, you practice a natural, attracting force.

You can't help but notice the results of Ki practices, whether done unconsciously, or consciously. This was a conscious practice, and the resulting flow of Ki noticeably brings more of the practitioner in the room, but only while they're practicing. As soon as the teacher stepped off the mat, the feeling in the room went back to normal.

To me now, after all these years, there is no such thing as normal. The ordinary is extraordinary, and my goal here is to show you ways and practices to keep that powerful sense of presence, may it follow you wherever you go. With or without ever having to enter a dojo, on or off the mat, enter your life, and welcome yourself to your *inner dojo.*

Once the demonstration got started, I wasn't sure if the student and teacher were faking. The student would run at him, and he would redirect their energy, completing technique with them "falling" gracefully like a stuntman.

Have you ever noticed how a stuntman falls? When someone falls in a movie, they roll diagonally, especially when they hit the ground hard, such as after being thrown out of a car.

As a visitor, this diagonal roll was the first thing we had to learn. We were going to take a tumble and though it didn't look real, we had to practice "fake falling" so we didn't splat on the mat.

The teacher's assistant, called the Uchi Deshi, which literally means the inside student, showed me how to roll. "Look at your back foot and roll forward with your arms making a circle, like you're holding a giant ball."

We had to practice by looking behind us while rolling forward. This is not what the body wants to do. I practiced rolling, however, and got fairly good at it. I never really nailed it like some practitioners, though, I never knew why. Later I found out this is because I have a moderately severe case of scoliosis.

I suppose taking a planned tumble saved my back from a lot of damage. I have fallen on cement, rolling nicely, instead of slipping. This came in handy when I was holding a baby in the snow.

During a practice where you're falling from a distance, sometimes from several feet in the air, splatting isn't an option. You can't fall on a hard surface day in and day out, without breaking down cartilage and bones.

I showed some kids a video of the practice and, because kids are candid, one said, "It looks like a bad movie." It does, and it did at the time. It took a while to understand what was real and what wasn't real in our dojo practice. I made that my personal project as I took an honest, closer look into this practice.

I was looking for something new when I ran into this little dojo. I had lost faith and started checking out emotionally. I hoped something could encourage me to stay connected in life.

The teacher there was small, but he had a huge presence, at least until he stepped off the mat and talked with the other students after class. When that happened, he gave off a weaker vibe, and also seemed a little unkind at times, even anti-social. "You have to be invited if you want to be a student here. You are not interviewing us; we are interviewing you. We'll let you know if you can join." I wondered why I kept coming back.

After a couple of days, I gave it another try. I wanted to see if there was anything to this Ki thing. As everyone waited silently and with full attention, the teacher entered the mat, and scanned over his students. He stopped at a blue belt, a young man worthy of demonstrating technique, and signaled him to come up to the center of the mat.

The student had to have the right "feeling" before being chosen. It was considered a great privilege to demonstrate technique with the Sensei. Having the right "feeling" turned out to be the most important technique one would ever learn to execute. I learned more about that later, but now, I was just trying to figure these people out.

He demonstrated what appeared to be a simple technique. With a Japanese vocabulary, he explained the movement, showed it twice, then bowed to the student who sat back down. He went on to try to clarify how to do the movements without using brute strength. "Try *not* to engage your muscle. That's harder for strong, athletic people to do. Much more difficult than it is for those who are weaker. Tough guys want to muscle their way through the movement when it doesn't work right away. They'll never get it if they force it. Try to stay soft, and use the momentum and strength of the other person. If you're doing it right, you should be able to execute effective technique by simply pointing your finger."

He showed the technique again with another student using just a finger, pointing the student in the direction he wanted them to go. This is only possible to do if the student runs towards the Sensei in an artificial looking "attack." Still, I wondered what was really happening with this "flow of Ki." Was there an element of reality to this practice? He then said to the class, "Now you try it." The students got up quickly and chose a partner.

It didn't' look difficult, and he certainly had explained it well enough. I thought it would be stupid-easy, but it also didn't look like it would ever happen in a real fight. "So far, I'm not impressed, but I'll play along" I thought to myself.

The students there seemed to be so enamored with the Sensei's abilities, I rolled my eyes, but only on the inside. "Find a partner," one of the students said, as they turned away and chose someone else.

I looked around and finally found someone who was looking back at me. I teamed up with her and gave it a try. Do you remember what to do? She didn't know either, and she was a yellow belt. Yellow belts had to have at least six months of practice, so I knew these movements were more complicated than they appeared. "At least I'll learn my left from my right," I reasoned, something I'd always struggled with, even when driving. I had no sense of direction, internally or externally, but it turns out the internal and external are inseparable.

I was taken aback by my mind's difficulty in recalling the details, surprised at my lack of body awareness. "Which way was I supposed to go? Was it under your arm? Left, right, which hand?" I felt so awkward, it reminded me of being the new kid at a job or in junior high. You know the feeling. It's never easy being the newbie, but I thought I could fake it and look kind of cool. I could not, I did not look cool.

The Sensei clapped twice, and everyone ran for a seat. They sat in a line, kneeling on their feet. The teacher walked past the line, pushing anyone who was behind or ahead back into place. The line had to be perfectly straight, with everyone sitting at attention. They gazed up at the teacher, their leader, waiting for another piece of his wise instruction. They looked like they were in love, giving full attention while they waited respectfully, hoping he would call on them. "Is this some kind of a cult?" As you can see, I was not part of this world, but why, I wondered, why do I keep coming back?

Later, I too found this sense of being "in love." What I loved was *my* Sensei, my only Sensei, which is Reality itself. I fell in love with life, my life, the people in it, the daily grind of it, all of this came alive, and I keep it alive through the inner practices. If I don't do that, I can coast on the momentum of previous mindfulness, but it starts to dry up and wind down. I need, and I believe we all need, a daily practice.

The reality you're stuck in now may not look lovely, or loveable, but it has to start there. If you don't see where you are now, it's not as easy to navigate the road ahead. I thought I saw where I was, but I was amazed to find, there is a deeper "seeing" when it comes to here and now.

While waiting for the teacher, one of the higher belts grabbed my hands. "Are you one of those fancy people who gets their nails done?" I wore makeup, but no fancy nails. Evidently, that was something that would bar me from practice. You might scratch someone, I suppose, but I had an attitude. No one likes being told what to do.

"No jewelry, clip and file your nails, and no garlic or onions for dinner," the assistant warned the class. "Sensei doesn't like the smell of your spicy foods."

One morning she walked in and sniffed, "I smell spices!" I can understand. I'm sure, walking around the room and working with people with smells pouring from their sweat, bringing what they had eaten into the room, that could be annoying. At the time, I was young, and I didn't like people telling me what to eat. Still, for some unknown reason, I stayed.

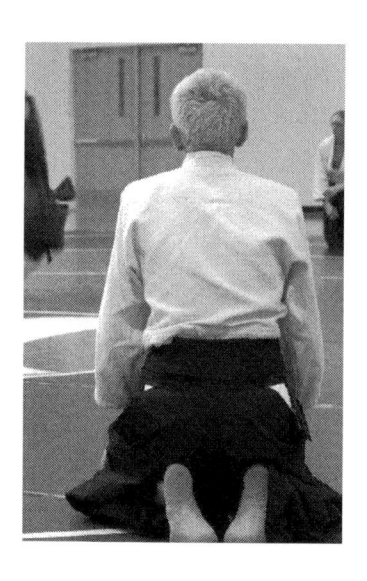

There were only about nine students at the dojo at one time. We sat "seiza" between practices. Seiza is just kneeling, sitting on your feet, which is no big deal until you've done it for a couple of hours.

Throughout the years, there never were a lot of students in these little dojo practices. People didn't get it, the Ki practice that is. It's not for everyone, but it is for me. I wasn't sure why I was there, but this little dojo ended up changing my life.

While I questioned the validity of the technique, I learned it well, and for this reason, I gained some genuine perspective about it over time. I learned about non-resistance, softness, using gravity, physical and emotional relaxation, and other forces of nature. Tension, power, and muscle take so much out of you by comparison. It took time to respect the art, but I got it after a few years.

Sometimes I would upset the Sensei's thoughts about what was real. I would test his idea that a person *had* to respond to Ki by simply not responding. This would throw him off, leaving him a little confused. Later, I understood why it was a good idea to respond to Ki, but I always knew it wasn't about control. While I had an appreciation and respect for his Ki, there were times he thought he could control the outcome like magic. I knew that was wrong, so I messed with him.

I know thoroughly that one can easily ignore Ki, but it isn't a good idea. I found out more about that through practice with the black belts.

Looking back, it's clear that being sensitive to Ki helps you feel what's coming. You should respond to a punch coming or see the balled-up fist before the punch or, even better, feel the anger that precedes the balled-up fist that comes before the punch, that is a good idea. It does seem smarter than waiting until you're punched in the face.

At that time, I had more respect for the kicking and punching martial arts. One of the blue belt students was in great shape. He was about 6'4, and he told me he had been a black belt in Taekwondo. "Is this stuff for real?" I asked him, "Couldn't you just punch or kick this guy, he looks kickable?" While he answered that he could, he also said that the Sensei would get him back, "He would probably do some kind of nasty technique back to me in retribution. It wouldn't be worth it." He was dead serious.

"Everybody make a circle with your index finger and thumb." The teacher explained, then he invited up a student to help him demonstrate. "Imagine your finger and thumb are separate, but pushing together with all your might, try to keep me from separating them." The student pushed hard, and the teacher separated his finger and thumb fairly easily.

"Imagine now that your finger and thumb are connected to your hand, whole, one piece. This time, your finger is connected to your thumb and they are working together. Fingers, hand, everything is one and connected to your center. Your center, which is one inch below your navel, is holding your finger and thumb together. Together with your whole body."

The Sensei used his own finger to trace the circle made by the students fingers. Round and round over the fingers he went, then starting slowly at first, he increased pressure, trying to separate the thumb from the finger, but this time it was difficult, almost impossible. "Now try it with a partner."

I stood there waiting for someone to choose me. "Crap, this is like choosing sides for baseball at school." Finally, I locked eyes with someone who was willing to help me.

I wasn't even a white belt yet, and these students preferred to work with those who were more experienced. I just didn't get it, and it made me feel like I was a burden. "This isn't like the Western, you pay, we please you, kind of practice. You have to earn your place here," one of the higher ups explained. That's not how I was brought up. We all have a place, but I get it, you don't owe me anything just because I'm a paying member.

This lovely young college kid approached me and took a bow, "Onegaishimasu." I looked puzzled. This person's smile seemed especially kind. "This is a polite Japanese phrase to say to one's opponent before engaging," she related, gently. It means, "I'm willing to work with you, or do your best, if you please, or I pray you, or "do me this favor." I tried to repeat the words and took a bow.

As she did the exercise with me, I wondered if she was really trying to pry my fingers apart. We took turns, and after some practice, I could see something real was going on. Maybe it was my muscles, or mindset, but something changed along with my thoughts. I was stronger when connected, and weaker when disconnected. My body and mind changed for the better or worse, depending on what I was thinking and feeling, and depending on connecting that to my bodily sensations.

It was my first physical demonstration, an introduction to the reality of the idea we've all heard. "What you think changes what you feel and *that* changes your body. Your reactions have an effect on the outcome."

When I thought the finger and thumb were separate, the muscle in the middle didn't engage. When I thought it was whole, the muscles changed in response. They fully engaged as a whole. My hand and fingers were one piece rather than separate pieces or muscles. "So, this is what is meant by the idea of becoming one with it?" No matter how hard she pulled, my finger's attachment to the whole made the movement powerful, much stronger than before, without any doubt.

This was just a glimpse into the powerful mind/body connection. It would be proven to me over and over again through many different techniques and practices. I would continue to strengthen my understanding of softness, wholeness, and connectedness as a strength.

I continue to learn these principles more competently as I go through my life applying them. I respond to pressure by relaxing deeply and softening completely, throughout stressful events and challenges. The more intense the stress, the more I sink into it, and deepen my relaxation response.

On the mat, the Sensei became more and more respected in my eyes. I never quite bought into the "worship teachers and previous teacher lineage" thing, but I became grateful for the teaching. There is something real about softness, connection, and the flow of Ki. This invisible life force is real.

Waking up to the softer, more subtle senses, brought a strange mixture of the practical and the magical into my life. It changed my interactions with physics, and it changed my life for the better.

The funny thing is, the results of practicing this way are absolutely repeatable. Though I couldn't apply the scientific method, I knew it was real, deeply and personally. I couldn't prove it, except to myself. Knowing this was enough to begin the process of feeling like I was more than just flesh and bone.

This knowledge was a kind of faith, and this faith filled some kind of need I was not even aware I had. I needed faith that I was more than just a lump of flesh, more than my body, but it had to be real. I didn't want it to be compensating for something untrue or lacking in my life.

When I saw that mind and body became stronger with soft practice, I felt hopeful. Not only does one become stronger connecting within, but it has an effect on other people outside the body, and beyond the body.

I went on to experiment with others, and learned the value of the sacred inner dojo. The practice of Ki should be tested with the world as your laboratory. I now do this practice internally, and through normal everyday movements. It is enough to get me past feeling hopeless about life. Our lives are bigger than the senses, and beyond the obvious. It brings me freedom from despair. Disciplined practice brings hope, and peace, and continues to do so, even through exceptionally difficult times. So much so, I want to try to put the experience into words, hoping I could be of help to you too.

Reality is the "Great Teacher." It is somewhat pliable, but I stay within its teachings, allowing it to flow through my mind and body, holding nothing back. I watch closely and trust completely that we are going somewhere. We are loved, and though it takes work, and we will take some steps backward, we are meant to spiral up, ever up, little by little.

As I entered into this practice wholeheartedly, I sat amazed while watching the teacher show examples of using Ki rather than physical strength. He showed honest ways to move minds and bodies out of the way, engaging the forces of nature, and using little, if any muscle at all. Of course, you need to engage some muscles, or you would just be a pile of jelly, but how little you need is absolutely amazing.

"You could be the strongest, toughest guy in a fight, but one day, someone will come along, someone stronger than even you. Maybe you'll get old, sick, or injured, but you may not always, you won't always be able to beat everybody up. So, what's the solution? You need to learn how to fight without using just your personal strength."

This Master Teacher wasn't the "Best in Show" when it came to Ki Aikido. Not everyone could see how good he really was. Without completing the training at the dojo where he was originally affiliated, he opened his own dojo. He was an outlier, some of the best of us are, and from my perspective, his teachings went further into reality than had previously been explored.

Finding another teacher like this would not be possible. I searched for someone honest, someone who didn't care about money or recognition, and someone that could teach with clarity. When I couldn't find a teacher, with wholehearted devotion, I opened a dojo and taught what I had been taught.

While I continued most of the traditions, I tried to bring in an element of Western respect for individualism. We all have different gifts to bring to the table, and we don't need commitment to tradition holding us back.

Tradition is a tool, and we stand on the backs of those who went before us, but that shouldn't make us *not look* reality in the face. While looking *at* reality, however, you also look through reality. I don't consider myself gullible, but I can see through the obvious to things unseen. There are invisible energy aspects, that can be proven, and that is a reality. Everything is energy, that's a real kind of vision too.

The teacher went on to demonstrate how to use the mind/body connection to increase strength from within. I was in love with the idea of an ethereal answer to inner and outer strength.

I became a real student, and bought my first gi, or dojo uniform. It had a smell that was a combination of bleach and sweat, and it was the sweetest smell, once this practice became my new habit. It turned out to be an effective method to stop fighting reality. It changed my busy, nagging mind and reduced resistance, which showed up as tension in my life.

In the first months of practice, I felt awkward, clumsy, and ineffective, not knowing my left from my right. After a while, however, I became noticeably graceful. For the first time ever, I could hear others whisper about my movements, "The higher the belt, the more grace I notice," commented one new student.

I moved with intention and movement became a beautiful thing. I still need a practice to keep grace in my movements. Without a constant practice, I start spilling things, losing things, and knocking into things fairly quickly.

I also learned about some internal qualities that needed revisiting. I didn't know how controlling I could be. I never thought of myself as a control freak.

I've seen stubbornness in the children I've worked with through the years. It is a common trait when one struggles with special needs. Do I really stiffen up and dig my heels in when under pressure? I did, it was a trained, ingrained response, and it was time to unlearn this reaction.

The Sensei's assistant stayed after class and taught me some of the deeper secrets of practice. She didn't mind sharing that I could be astutely aware, and unaware alternatively. While my awareness would be fully checked in at times, I checked out fully as well, losing consciousness and going thoroughly on auto-pilot.

We do that as humans. We check in and out, in and out, it's normal that our attention fluctuates. My awareness, however, was extremely bumpy.

The class was happy to help me with the complicated technique, but they don't let you in on the secrets of self-defense until you've proven yourself to be in the right frame of mind. That's a good idea. You don't want the wrong people to know the right moves.

The assistant respected that I was powerful, except when things got difficult for me. When that happened, she turned to me and said, "Do you notice you try to control things when you're losing?

Controlling, stubborn, aggressive? While these attributes are normally associated with strength and, compared to a withdrawn victim mentality, they might get a leg up on "being nice," but in reality, they are a weakness.

Making yourself a mighty wall gives others something to push up against. When you don't budge, when you're impossible to move, you are not reaching this goal of inner and even outer strength. Being tough, rough, and "in your face," is not anywhere near strong enough to handle what comes next. This is not real and lasting strength.

When awareness took a sharp nosedive downward, I became annoyingly controlling. What an insight! Controlling behavior is at the core of abuse, and it is the key to most problems in our culture today.

When Harrison Ford was asked about, "The Force" in his Star Wars movies he said, "Force Yourself." This is the key to getting away from abusive, unbalanced behavior. Force yourself, control yourself. Controlling and forcing others is a weakness.

I was always so nice, and never saw myself as controlling, but nice can be controlling too. It's a way of controlling perception, i.e. "You have to perceive me in this particular way, because I'm so nice." The Uchi Deshi read clear past my outwardly kind demeanor and said, "You're going to get your butt kicked. Take that energy down a notch, or you'll get into a fight."

At twenty-seven years old, I wasn't looking for a fight, and didn't live in a bad neighborhood, but what I didn't know was how hard life would push me. It would have shoved me around with my own controlling nature if I hadn't learned another way. This "Art of Peace" practice was and is the "other way."

It took me a while to understand what she was reading. I really am a decent person, overall, pretty nice, and generally good, but when others saw through me clearly, I realized I had some inner changes to make, some learning to do.

This energy the assistant, and all of the higher belt students were reading was called, "The Feeling."

"The Feeling" was central and critical in our dojo teachings. It is energy in general. It is also the energy one is emanating as they approach you, or it can be the energy a practitioner is sending out.

In the words of the founder of Aikido, Morihei Ueshiba, you may gain some understanding of this strange, golden feeling. Through it, one can convey a sense of pervasive peace. The following quote is from a spiritual experience Morihei Ueshiba had. After this experience, his martial arts skills increased significantly.

But before I quote him, let me explain the word he uses, "Budo."

These words, bu and do, are Japanese words that are rich in meaning. To keep it simple for now, the word "bu" means military or martial and "do" means way. Budo would basically mean the martial way. Some familiar examples of the word "do" might be, dojo, place to practice the martial way, Judo, the soft, flexible way, Aikido, the way of energy in harmony. The word "Ki" in Aikido is synonymous with energy.

In this life changing experience, Morihei Ueshiba said,

"At that moment I was enlightened: the source of Budo is God's love — the spirit of loving protection for all beings ... Budo is not the felling of an opponent by force; nor is it a tool to lead the world to destruction with arms. True Budo is to accept the spirit of the universe, keep the peace of the world, correctly produce, protect and cultivate all beings in nature."

When we talk about "the feeling," we mean that you have a "feeling" and that it is palpable. It comes out of your fingers and pours out of every cell of your body. Increasing "the feeling" leans you towards peace because it calls you ever closer towards empathy.

As a student learning about Ki, you increase the feeling or sensation of this energy in your own body. You learn to increase your sensitivity to the feeling or energy others carry with them as well.

Having something more than flesh and bone radiating off of your body is not magic, and it isn't anything new. With practice, however, the feeling can be intensified through unblocking yourself.

Because of our generations of conditioning, we are insensitive to Ki. We get this feeling back with specific awareness practices that undo this conditioning.

You've heard people talk about how a dog senses fear? You may know of this firsthand. This is because they are tuned into something more than the object you call your body. The dog feels your energy, and this dog didn't practice martial arts. Dogs, like most of the rest of nature, are just more primal, and so they are not blocking "the feeling."

You can feel the energy of a dirty look, or a room that has residual energy after an argument. "The tension was so thick you could cut it with a knife." You've heard that, and you have felt it too.

Sensitivity to energy can start by simply paying attention a little bit more. You begin with increasing awareness by picking up on expressions and body language. You can then tune in even further, trying to be aware of micro-expressions and other subtle "tells" that speak about what someone is feeling. These subtleties seep into your unconscious even when they're not overtly noticed. When they become conscious, these micro-social-cues are more obvious.

Soon, as your attention skills expand, you build attention muscle or **Ki**. You will find this attention takes you further into sensitivity to "the feeling." You start with obvious communication and move towards that ethereal "something more." It is through the senses, rather than instead of the senses, that you increase "the feeling."

This feeling is a force. It consists of the fullness of tuning into what is, and then some. Sensitivity to the feeling and the energy around you is normal, but it is also useful. You can practice it and enhance it.

Then learn to sense it coming in and flowing out even more.

You can learn to send the feeling out from your body, through your fingertips and onto another person. It's not voodoo or magic, it's just that there's something real in the energy around and about your body. You can play with it as you learn to feel this energy coming at you. It's in everyone and everything, we all have it. Some would say, "yeah right," while others would say "of course."

Most cultures in the East believe in this life force energy and it is simply commonplace. While it's called Prana in India, Chi in China, and Ki in Japan, there's no word for it in Western culture except perhaps, awareness or presence.

You cannot override the will of others with "the feeling" or the ability to sense it and manipulate it, but it is influential. It's a powerful force, but, if you think you can use it to control anyone, especially in a competitive fight, intending to show off your power, you're 'bout to get your butt kicked.

Getting good at increasing your bodily sensation, which increases others being able to read you, is a matter of movement, awareness, and transparency.

This is why being candid and readable is also powerful. It has an effect on the world around you, and the feeling you carry with you. That makes *all* of your experiences more fascinating and more fun.

Try these simple awareness practices to begin to feel the life force increase within you:

1. Feel your fingers as you reach for anything, such as a vacuum handle, a piece of paper or a bite to eat. Send an invisible feeling into the

object, like you're touching it before you actually do touch it.

2. Practice sending a feeling out by opening up your body through dance. Move with chest out and arms open. Wide open, fluid and swinging movements work best.

3. Before you enter someone else's space for a friendly conversation, imagine they can feel you enter, and may even be able to tell what you're thinking and feeling.

4. Move with the other in slight, unnoticeable mirrorlike movements. When they shift their legs or make an expression, mimic it, but try not to get caught. It will seem weird, but it will connect you.

5. Play with this "force" through body awareness until you can feel your body tingle. Rest with your palms

up and feel the spaces between your fingers and toes. Feel your fingertips and each toe individually.

These are examples of how to step up "the feeling," and they will also help you detect it more clearly in others with practice. These are moving, living, exercises that make life better.

Increased sensation, and therefore, increased Ki, isn't intended to help you win in a fight, mentally or physically. That is never the point. The point is the power and rightness of awareness itself. It is a healing force.

The awareness that is infused into Ki is soft, supple, agile and strong. It has a voice, but its voice is silent. More a language of the heart. If it actually talks to you, that's not "the feeling." That's something you wrap up in a paper towel and flush down the toilet, ha-ha.

While there is value in all martial arts for different reasons, this one in particular, this inner Aikido, when using Ki, gets you to flow.

You can do this, get to flow, if you keep a quiet mind while you practice moving in dancelike rhythm to music, or throughout the day as you go about your usual routine.

We call the practice of fluid movements, "*moving meditations.*" These meditations have a liquidlike, peaceful feeling that brings you more present, closer to empathy, and closer to your own nature.

When it comes to fighting in the Octagon, or MMA, Aikido has received some harsh feedback recently. I believe this is because it is not a combative martial art. My teacher would say, "If you want self-defense, get a gun." Aikido is *not* an MMA or Brazilian Jujitsu, you lose, I win, kind of a fighting art.

Don't get me wrong, I respect the fighting arts and practice them as well. We had a karate expert and Okinawan weapons teacher, as well as a fantastic group of Gracie Brazilian Jujitsu practitioners teach in our dojo.

Fighting in a ring needs to be effective, but this form of Aikido is not really about fighting. Its intention is to move hearts and minds. Aikido's teachings are real, and can be effective, but they cannot compare to these other martial arts in a brawl. In fact, it's called, "The Art of Peace."

Art of Peace? How can a martial art be called an art of peace? Because this martial art moves in harmony with an attacker and changes their intention if possible. The hope is to dissipate anger without causing more injury than absolutely necessary. The intention is to move the attacker closer to peace.

The movements of Ki Aikido, specifically, are soft, smooth and peaceful. They teach the practitioner about empathy through a language of motion, much like Tai Chi, but with more dynamic and dancelike movements.

These movements don't look tough. They're not meant to be used to show off. They work best when actually fighting, but even then, it's more about the feeling than the technique. In life, no one usually comes at you running. The momentum used in an Aikido dojo is artificial, but it is teaching, though on the downlow, about things not easily grasped.

Ai, harmony, Ki, energy, and Do, the way or path. Aikido is the way of energy in harmony. This is what you're doing with this book. You are doing inner Aikido. A mental version of using your energy in harmony with the energy of others.

Here is a peek into some of the dojo practice secrets:

1. **Keep One Point** – One point is also called your center. You've heard of the idea of being centered, but what is your center? It's deep within your lower abdomen where there is no tension whatsoever.

    In martial arts and in many other arts such as acting, singing, and dancing, using your center makes you more powerful and present.

    Your center is located one inch below the navel. The center is in the fulcrum or midpoint of the body, a pivot point like the center of a seesaw. Think, speak and move from there. If you're not sure what that means, it's not important. No matter where you focus in your body, at least you're not in your head.

    Most people live much of their lives in their heads. Attention on what's in the head is how the mind gets caught up in the ever-flowing stream of thought. This constant inner chatter has a powerful undertow which drags you down beneath your best judgement and your best self.

Your lower abdomen or your gut is considered to be the most effective, whole-body place from which to think, act, and live.

You can get to your one point or center by placing your hand on your lower abdomen. Breathe through this area and "think" from there. As you breathe, allow your emotions to rise and fall like the ocean tide. This quote has the perfect words for the feeling.

> "Consider the ebb and flow of the tide. When waves come to strike the shore, they crest and fall, creating a sound. Your breath should follow the same pattern, absorbing the entire universe in your belly with each inhalation."
>
> ~ Morihei Ueshiba

2. **Physically Relax Completely** – This is self-explanatory but there are exercises to intensify your ability to relax while also keeping one point and extending Ki. See more at the end of the book under exercise number nine, Rag Doll.

3. **Keep Weight Underside** – This is more difficult to explain. The exercises in relaxing will get you there too. In fact, all these principles lead to the same state, or at least aid each other. Doing one leads to successfully doing the other. Practice it with a friend and see if you can increase its effect.

   We would hold each other's arms up and then let go. Our partner's job is to relax and allow their arms to drop to their sides, limp. Then, using just enough muscle to hold them up, we would test to be sure their weight distributed under their arms, like a heavy bag of water.

If you're doing it right, when someone bumps your elbow while you're holding a drink, it won't spill.

Don't worry if this doesn't make sense. If you're relaxing completely, you are also keeping your weight underside.

4. **Extend Ki** - This means putting yourself out there or extending energy outwards. I am naturally an introvert, many of us are. No one would know this if they met me on the street. I put myself out there so much that this practice has become a habit, and the habit of extending myself is so ingrained, it is now part of my personality.

To extend Ki, imagine there is light pouring out of your fingertips as they are pointing towards the ceiling. Imagine that when you wiggle your fingers, they touch the ceiling. It's as if they were lightsabers.

You can also imagine water pouring out of your hands. More like a fire hose than the trickle of a faucet. This puts energy into your fingers, and you should begin to feel them tingle. Imagine that tingle flows through the body of someone willing to practice with you. This is called, "sending Ki." Ask them if they can feel it.

While practice does some strange and powerful things to the way you use your body, if you want to use that power to cause a problem, it's the Sensei's job to straighten you out.

I remember a time when I was showing off and needed an attitude adjustment. While using a technique called, "bridge," I was working with a new white belt student. I was playing with her energy, because it was interesting, but it wasn't the way I was supposed to be practicing.

The idea in bridge is to get down on all fours and make a bridge. Your partner then leans on you. At the same time, while they're resting with all they've got on your back, they are trying to hold their balance. When you drop to the floor, they should still be standing, centered, and stable, though in a bent position.

I was having fun, picking up the new student's energy and making her fall. It was fascinating to me that this was a real thing. I was amazed at the process of moving energy around. I proved its reality to myself by playing with this energy, but I wasn't thinking of how I made the new student feel.

The last time she tumbled onto the floor with me, it caught the attention of my teacher from across the room. When he looked over at me, I knew I was in trouble.

The Sensei walked over casually and acted like he was teaching how to do the bridge technique to the new student. He asked me to get down on all fours to demonstrate. I centered myself, knowing what was coming, and made a bridge. My Sensei then positioned himself over me with both palms on my back. He pushed with all his weight and might.

The weird thing was, centering myself beforehand really worked. When I bounced back up like a spring, he looked surprised. He said to the white belt, "That wasn't supposed to happen, usually they splat." I still got the point. I woke up sore from head to toe the next day, as well as a little embarrassed.

Your automatic response of hardness, butting up against someone who has dug their heels in deep, means a confrontation of hardness against hardness. This is how we injure ourselves and others.

When being authentic means you have to speak up, proceed with caution. You may feel like someone needs protecting because they're being bullied. This is a worthy cause, so come to their defense. But when it comes to protecting an ideal, such as a religion, that is going to require patience and softness.

If you're right about your ideals, you won't be in a rush to prove them. You should be able to proceed with an open discussion that does not include any fear or hardness.

If you are to have any influence, feel your way through it gently. You want to speak up from a place inside yourself that is peaceful, powerful, and *yielding,* rather than fearful. Move sensitively and give way to their energy rather than going for a direct hit. If you soften your stance, presenting your ideas will have a stronger impact.

You will know your intentions are hardline if you feel you're in a hurry. This inner push or need to convince someone of anything at all is a weakness. You know you're right and they are obviously dead wrong. You feel like you're talking to an idiot, and you can prove it. This is hardness.

Listen, hear, feel, relate, and connect. Don't run from it, and don't go on the attack. Resist the temptation to call anyone wrong. Even if they are wrong, and even if they know that, if you say it directly, they will resist you rather than learn from you.

Softening yourself does not betray your sense of authenticity, but rather it adds to it, because you really don't know. You might know the facts, but you don't know everything about what this person needs, why they are so stubborn, or how it is that they can't see the truth when it's so clear to you.

Since you really don't know, be authentic, but be curious, dig in deeper and ask whatever comes to mind, but avoid calling them wrong. To quote the father of public speaking, Dale Carnegie,

"I am convinced now that nothing good is accomplished and a lot of *damage* can be done if you tell a person straight out that he or she is wrong."

We actually learn much more from "wrong people" than we do from those who agree with us. If we are to be a positive and influential force in the lives of others, we need further training. Since, we are in training, we need an "opponent." Without an opponent willing to stand in opposition, how can we test that training, and our peacemaking abilities?

It sounds a lot like sensitivity training, but rather than teaching the other to be more sensitive, you're teaching them to feel what they cause others to feel. When you feel the pain that *you* are causing, you tend to be more careful about what you say and do.

When someone considers themselves empathetic, sometimes it

means they're insecure or lack a sense of humor. It's no fun being around people who get hurt easily.

Empathy shouldn't interfere with the fun, but it is a fine line. One has to be able to care and not care in all the right places. That takes practice, learning, and feedback.

If you introduce a shy person to speaking up gradually, they'll soon see more clearly when it comes to their own insecurities. As they get to know themselves better, they'll have a chance to become more resilient just by getting more interaction in general.

I remember seeing a shy and damaged monkey who wouldn't play with the others. He clung to the bars in a corner of the cage and kept his head down. The other monkeys teased him and smacked him out of his withdrawn state. Soon he joined them in the fun and play.

Now I'm not calling my husband a monkey, really, but when I met him, this is just what he did. I was a little shy and withdrawn. He teased me relentlessly until I finally gave up on getting my feelings hurt. I gained a better sense of humor and tougher skin because of him.

We are polar opposites, but we learn from each other. He still makes me laugh, though he often goes too far. Because of our influence on each other, I am rarely oversensitive, and he is more empathetic. I can even appreciate his heartless nature, usually, haha, but he is actually more empathetic than me under some circumstances, such as listening to boring people.

Just being around other people who are honest with themselves, people who don't "punish" you by getting their feelings hurt, helps everyone to relax and have a sense of humor.

With empathy, others care about us when things really do get tough, but they don't have to worry about everything they say. We can take it when we're teased, and we can learn to handle some honest feedback.

Honesty without concern for rejection helps shy people to speak up, but what is shyness? When you're quiet, some people think you're stuck up or secretly judging them. Who knows? Maybe they fear that they don't have anything interesting to say. Maybe they fear that *you* are going to judge *them*.

Either way, if you find that someone is exceptionally shy, just get them to talk by using a few words to begin with. They should be able to come up with a few simple sentences, but you can help them if they're struggling.

It's fun to pry a quiet person open. You might be surprised to find out just what's been going on inside their heads. You might find something quirky and fun, or you might be sorely afraid. Perhaps they're not so likeable and they've been thinking horrible things.

Whether or not you like someone, you can still understand them. If you work to strengthen the sense of empathy in others, you contribute to a better world.

Children are almost always naturally empathetic. They are entertaining because they don't fear speaking candidly. They haven't learned about being judged. Shy adults, once they open up, might get used to speaking candidly too.

We're all complicated, and difficult in some way or another but, have you ever wondered what the world would look like if we had to feel what we caused others to feel? It would be the end of criminal intent.

When you run into a problem, you can help others stay soft by following guidelines in "The Peacemaking Practice."

One person at a time, usually the one with unbalanced feelings, goes first. The problem should be completely heard and understood before the other presents their side or alternative perspective.

Peacemaking Practice

1. Choose the situation they would like to address.
2. Identify how they feel about it i.e. sadness, anger, worry – help them get creative with their adjectives.
3. Talk about what they need from the other to feel better. "I have a need for safety, freedom of speech, or to be seen and heard."
4. Have them make a clear request without placing blame or fault on the other person.

5. Ask the person to repeat back what was said using their own words. What did they say about what they feel, what they need, and what they're requesting from the other?
6. Both people take turns doing this until the situation is resolved. Don't forget to ask questions to further your understanding of what the other person needs and is requesting.
7. The one who first started the process needs a response and acknowledgement before the other can move forward. Will they do what was requested? Why or why not? This has to be cleared up before the other can take their turn.

Ugh, hashing out details can take so long. And, what is so off putting about talking in terms of needs and feelings?

Rebellion may be cool in the movies, but in reality, it's worse than useless. Just as it is with people pleasing, both the rebel and the compliant person are not finding their own voice. The rebel is seeking to do the opposite of what *you want*. The people pleaser is complying with what *you want*. Which of these is addressing what *they want?*

People feel your vulnerable, authentic presence. Your nature has an edge, but it's not rebellious or constantly agreeing and being, "good."

Psychological words like "needs" and "feelings" don't sit well with a lot of people, including most teenagers, but relational intelligence depends on the use of these words. This is what I think Socrates meant by, "Know Thyself." Know what you feel, and what you need.

The following are Moving and Stillness Practices and Meditations for Inner Radiant Peace

These inner practices are unusual and effective if you apply them. I know this through rigorous personal testing on the mat as a martial arts instructor for over 25 years.

Rather than reading through them all, it's best to read only one week at a time, write about it, and then let it all seep in.

These exercises are meant to make permanent changes in your perception and in your life. Moving slowly helps you absorb them fully.

Over time, there will be a real difference in your magnetic, radiant sense of peace. Your ability to pull in closer all that which inspires you, will increase beyond measure.

You will notice other people will feel that difference, they may not be able to put it into words, but they will feel it. The more you practice, the more your radiant awareness will increase inner peace. Watch stress and anxiety dissipate as your true nature shines through, like it does in early childhood.

Devote yourself to this process completely, which works to reveal more of *you*. It is you. You are accepting and welcoming yourself. Abandon yourself to the real you. Allow yourself to see clearly and you will uncover the next best step in receptivity to the natural peace and flow of your true nature.

The entry point is *not* wandering from where your body is in space and time. This can be especially difficult. Allow and let go, take it all in, and watch thoughts float by without fighting them. Let yourself flow with ease while you watch the process with pen and paper ready. This helps you not to succumb to the constant flow of thought.

Throughout the process, beware that your mind will do anything to convince you to wander off into a daydream. It will do dances, pull tricks, and make up urgent needs. There is rarely, however, a need to go into the future or past.

If you do wander into thought, keep a journal, and write about it. That way your mind isn't taking you away from yourself. Writing things down is still here and now.

Writing everything down will bring radiant clarity in retrospect. I use the word radiant because awareness has a golden, radiant quality about it. Just observe honestly, quietly, and you will see an improvement in yourself and in the dynamic of your relationships.

Week One: Starting Point Where You Are

If you want a better experience of your reality, know it better, *as it is now*, more fully, first. Acceptance is the first step towards lasting change. This may sound obvious, but I have some unusual ways to deepen acceptance. It works if you work it.

One example of an effect from a particular practice is that you can slow time down. When you do this, you see what's coming. When you see what's coming, you have more choices in view before that hits you in the face.

There are many layers to consider, so it's not as clear cut as it may appear to be at first. On one level, you already attention. Maybe you don't struggle with attention deficit, but there are always

ways to dig in even deeper into new and undiscovered layers.

In the same way attention deficit causes negative consequences, digging down into the moment to pay *ever more* attention, has payoffs.

On some level, your mind wanders. Everyone's attention wavers in and out, oscillating like the breath, the ocean tide, and the rhythm of a heartbeat. It's only human but, if you can get those moments when you are "*in*" closer together, you'll be paying "Super-Attention." This super-attention gets results.

The ocean is choppy on the surface, though still and quiet in its depths. Like this, there is a place within you where it is absolutely silent. There, you feel deeply calm and quiet. When you find this place deep below your busy mind, stillness emerges, and with it comes clarity. The more you can get to this level of mind, the more pathways you find to get there quickly, even in times of trouble.

With clarity, you level up naturally. There is no coasting, you either spiral up or you spiral down. When meditations and other practices are worked deep into your life, your life becomes a living, moving meditation.

Given a chance in quietness, trust arises. This will make good things bubble up to the surface of your mind and your life.

When you're able to get beyond the loud noise of emotions, thoughts, fears, and unsettling feelings, you find the energy to pay attention more deeply. Through this, you will see real transformation appear in every aspect of your life, making it ever better.

This week, practice to increase attention to the point of Super-Attention. One way to do this is to say, under your breath, "see, hear, feel, see hear feel," like a mantra, over and over again.

The mind is comfortable with your ingrained patterns, so it will work ridiculously hard to distract you from your new focus. This mantra will begin the process of freeing your mind and, with this kind of focus, you will dismantle the obstacles in the way of your peace.

Reality is more malleable through knowing it, and through knowing yourself well. Who are you?

What does life want from you? You will realize more and more who you really are, and why it is that YOU are needed, the *real you.* Life, Reality, wants to cultivate who your truest nature.

See, hear, and feel everything Reality offers. Feel more and more at ease with your current Reality because *it is* your Great Teacher, your Sensei, if you will.

Once you are in sync with that, moving your Reality closer to your deepest self-knowledge becomes easier with each practice session.

The art of a good practice is like clicking on an icon, it magnifies and uncovers new perspectives, higher levels of truth.

Get feedback through face-to-face interactions with other people. This will reveal the results of your weekly practice. Use this feedback to test your methods and to propel your weekly ascent to higher levels of awareness, i.e. higher dimensions. Every wave of emotion is a place, a dimension, where you live more fully or not, depending on your level of acceptance.

After practice, sleep on it. Allow space between each session to do the work for you.

Time and space after practicing seeing, hearing, and feeling everything, moves your mind and body further into reality. This gives your mind and emotions a chance to strengthen the connections that serve you best, with each passing day.

With this practice, over time, you arrive at a higher-dimensional state of mind, and you stay there. This is a place in which you know just what to do. In martial arts, this place is called, "Spontaneous Right Action."

If for some reason, you should have planned for something, but didn't, you may find yourself in a situation or inner place, where your safety feels precarious. This is the root cause of anxiety.

If this happens, it's too late for planning, the next, most effective choice is to be fully alert and relaxed. Switch into a primal mode.

This mode is pure presence, and it is a "place" in which all the rest of creation lives. Now that our cognitive connections are internally established, humans must re-learn what it means to be present, fully observant, and alive.

Even plants communicate on a primal level, alert to the presence of a passerby.

Write about what has improved through the discipline of seeing, hearing, and feeling everything, being aware of the presence vibrating in all things, but without thinking. Do this especially during repetitive daily tasks.

Week Two: Rag Doll Physically Relax Completely

Telling yourself to relax physically, talks to your mind and spirit. This may seem obvious, but it's *through* the normal and mundane, that you find extraordinary secrets. Increase the usual relaxation response, noting how often you tense up and where tension is located in your body. Then, if you can't emotionally relax, you can deliberately, physically relax ever deeper. This helps your emotions. Practice it when it doesn't matter, and this practice will come back to help you when it does matter. Body relaxation done so often it is your second nature, speaks. It whispers deep into your worry, "Say yes to life, everything is acceptable."

Sometimes you may find yourself resisting life. When you do this, it will show up as physical and mental tension. This tension will clog up your sense of flow. If you relax completely, and regularly, you unblock yourself. You allow who you really are to flow more freely through your body.

This flow has attractive, magnetic power. It brings you more of what you genuinely want from life. You are holding tension more often than you are likely to be aware. Scan your body, and when you do, relax micro-tensions deliberately. You'll feel more and more like yourself, your best self, your truest self.

You don't need to become anything different from who you are. You only need to uncover the *truth* of who you are.

Like the acorn holds all the cellular information for what the oak tree is destined to be, all that you are destined to be is held in your cells. Unlock what that is by feeling the tingling sensation in your cells. Allow that to flow freely.

When you open the channels and let yourself pour through your body, unresisted, you won't become something you're not. You won't become a high profile actor, Gandhi or Mother Theresa. You can only become more you, and that's just what we need.

We need you. Life needs the real You. Without developing yourself into the fullness of all you really are, we unconsciously miss you. You are a missing piece of life's puzzle, and that leaves a void. Relax into yourself, and you will fill that void. You, the real you, this is what life wants. What a lovely discovery!

When you want to stop reality from being what it is, the natural effect is stress. This stress can be counteracted through a relaxation practice. One of those practices is called, "Rag Doll."

A rag doll practice is a martial art practice. This is because being loose and relaxed is more powerful. It also makes you less likely to get injured, much like a drunk is less likely to get injured in a car accident.

First, act like a limp, loose drunk. As different areas of your body tighten up, overexaggerate the drunk-like movements, and shake off the tension. This is a fun exercise!

We often hold much of our tension in the neck and shoulders. This is because it's in the shoulders we attempt to carry the weight of the world.

Are there any other areas where you hold tension? Relax them completely and deliberately by walking around the room, flopping like a rag doll.

Written and framed on the wall in my dojo where I taught many of these practices were the words, "Relax Completely." We would laugh as we walked around the dojo like drunken toddlers, trying to relax every bone and muscle. Of course, you have to have some tension, or you'd be a pile of jelly, but we relaxed as deeply as possible, allowing gravity to suck out any unnecessary tension.

When you walk around like a floppy rag doll, let gravity do most of the work. Let your arms fall to your side. You can also let someone else hold your hands and arms up for you. When they let go, do your arms flop down to your side? If not, you're holding tension in your arms and shoulders.

Do this "rag doll" practice for just a few minutes a day throughout your week. Note what happens to your mind, your choices, and the way you feel in general. It may allow feelings through that you've been holding down, but when they come up, you can deal with them, and change them more consciously.

Tuning into your body's position in relation to the things around you, called proprioception, becomes enhanced with this relaxation practice. The perception grows like a muscle.

Next, tune into areas of tension in your body. Squeeze muscles tight, hold that feeling for seven seconds, then relax them completely, letting go of your tension as you exhale. Do this with every muscle, including the tiny muscles in your facial expressions, between your brow and around your mouth, and so on.

Give it some time through the week and see what happens. Your brain noticeably makes more space for your practiced perceptions such as complete relaxation. Now relaxation is more automatic, and you won't even have to think about it.

When you relax completely, you say to your mind, through your body's relaxation response, that there is nothing to fear. No need to worry.

You also speak to others through your relaxed body language. You remind them to relax with you. A relaxed body, one that is not stuffing energy down, has a powerful voice. It is an effective transmitter of information, and it is louder than the thoughts of others. The likelihood of them responding to you instinctively will greatly increase when you are completely relaxed.

When you don't tighten up, you are in tune with the forces of nature, including your own nature. You can feel where you are going, the direction your reality is headed, and you can redirect it if necessary or desirable.

You can even help others by being relaxed. They can feel it and they will naturally relax with you. You also help them ease their own negative energy, such as jealousy or animosity.

Life and other people will continue to give you tests and challenges. This is a good thing because it's only through adversity that you can test yourself and up your game.

One recent challenge was insightful. A friend became emotionally unbalanced because of a controversial political statement made by another.

Rising up out of his center, (more on this later) he had to consciously relax his body to ease his mind. This had a positive effect on the interaction and saved him from undoing the progress they had made in the relationship.

You'll need to train yourself with repetition if you're going to be able to relax under pressure. Train yourself to respond to tension by relaxing even deeper.

Week Three: Keep Your One Point

You have heard about being centered. Did you know that there is a way to test whether or not you are physically centered?

When you are centered, it doesn't only apply to your physical centeredness. If you are centered physically, you are also spiritually, mentally, and emotionally centered at the same time. Mind and body are inseparably connected.

To find if you're centered, first find a friend. They will help test your center. It may take some practice to find this sturdy place within your abdomen, so try not to feel discouraged if it doesn't work the first time. Keep at it, and never give up.

Stand with your shoulders relaxed and shake out all your tension. Hold the palm of your hand over your abdomen just below the navel. Next, ask your friend to gently push you on the shoulder, testing your sense of balance at the core.

As you move your attention from the top of your head to this area of your abdomen, just feel what happens to your balance.

Everyone is at least partially balanced, or we would all be constantly falling. For this reason, allow yourself to really feel what happens to your balance without trying to catch yourself. What do you experience when your focus is on the top of your head, and then what happens when you change your focus to your abdomen? With practice, you should start to feel an increasing, though subtle difference.

You won't want to fall, so you'll naturally try to resist going off balance. Just feel the slight sensation of falling, but ask your partner to be sure and catch you if you start to stumble. Then go back and forth between what happens when you focus on the top of your head as opposed to putting your focus on the area in your abdomen, one inch below your navel.

It's not a pushing contest, so your partner should not be trying to push you over. They are there to help you feel for a mild change in your sensation of balance.

After a while, you'll feel an immovable, solid core. You don't want to dig your heels in, however. Move naturally when someone pushes too hard. Toro! When they push too hard, get out of the way, and throw *them* off balance.

Thinking and moving from the center of your body is called "Keeping One Point." The person you're asking to test you can come from all angles. They may try to throw you off balance when coming from behind, then from the side, and then in front of you.

The person testing your balance should start by pushing very gently while slowly increasing the pressure. This will help you to get a feel for your core strength. See if you hold your position (stay centered) while they push other areas besides your shoulders as well. They can test your arms, your ankles, and so on. They can also try to scare you with a sudden, loud noise, and test again. Sink into the feeling without resistance. Relax even deeper and see if your partner can feel a solid core, while you stay put.

What makes you lose your balance? This is a fun way to play with your physical centeredness. You'll become stronger and more agile.

To sink further into your center, try to feel the gravity beneath you, try to allow it to pull on your relaxed arms and body. When you lift your arms, allow them to drop to your side. Imagine they are bags of water with the weight falling naturally to the underside of your arms. We call this "Keeping weight underside."

In our martial arts classes, students would have fun testing each other after class. For example, when a student would lift the glass to take a drink, another student would shove his elbow. If the student wasn't centered, with their weight on the underside of their arms, they would spill their drink.

This may sound strange but try to think from your belly throughout the week. Notice your sensations as you place your hand on your abdomen. Re-center yourself frequently while you do normal, everyday tasks.

Write about what changes you notice. What happens? Are you more aware of your center? Do you feel happier or see things more clearly? This will happen if you stay with it and make it a daily habit.

Week Four: See Right Through You - Transparency

You can make yourself open, with a sense of relaxed vulnerability, using body language and practices. Vulnerability is attractive, sweet, organic, and it reveals your true nature. It may feel as if you are unprotected and exposed, but this is actually the energy of receptivity. Being receptive is a monumental superpower.

Again, start with the physical aspect of the practice. Rather than folding your arms, or crossing your legs, step into the space between you and another. Not just another with romantic intentions, but any other being whose energy feels right and cozy. You can, in a sense, fall in love with and open up to every being placed in your path.

Talking close with love for a child, a pet, or a wild animal, you open to a relationship that is sacred. Your beautiful face, your lovely body, your smooth and easy gaze, and your anticipation, you are something amazing that is about to happen to someone else.

Be open and vulnerable to that. It will have a profound effect on all of your connections, as well as your overall energy.

Start with your body stance and position. Your body will teach your mind. Open your arms, metaphorically on the inside, as you interact with others. Feel your tingling, alive body, every cell bathed in comfortable awareness, making a spiritual connection.

When you are transparent, others are more responsive to your thoughts, feelings, and intentions. The more open and real your thoughts and feelings, the more of an effect you have on others. This is because people can feel authenticity.

The more practice under your belt, the more intense the effect. This is because you are getting to know your "wild-child" self more intimately. Believing *that* will make it happen even more intensely.

The placebo effect is like this. If the patient believes a sugar pill will work, it's more likely to work. If the doctor prescribing the placebo believes in it too, this increases its effectiveness.

To get to your truest, most open self, try thinking one way, and then another. See how your thoughts create feelings. Keep trying different perspectives out until those feelings begin to feel ever more real, more you.

See how testable your effect can be on others through feedback. This is not manipulation. What could be less manipulative than being openly vulnerable?

Part of what's happening when you see responsiveness to your openhearted body-mind has to do with changes in our body language. There are imperceptible micro-expressions, and a feeling that radiates from your body-mind, that help you relate to another, and bring out the best in them.

Like the placebo effect, what you think, and how you believe potentially changes the outcome of their perception. The more transparent, the more intensely effective.

To be a more effective, "mind mover," you can rely upon your sense of compassion. Move and play with your own emotions, not those of another.

If you use your energy to manipulate or control others, it will bring ugly close to your life, and things can turn ugly fast. When you see you're having a powerful influence on someone, move them only towards that which benefits everyone involved. This keeps your energy pure, radiant, and transparent.

Bring to a relationship a sense of newness, openness, raw honesty, kindness, and vulnerability. This is actually an immensely powerful state of being. When you are open, it tends to open others, so look back at them deeply. See who they are, and be honest. Are you a good emotional match?

Newness of mind and body put you in the right frame of mind, *in that moment.* This frame of mind creates an unusually powerful connection. You also need the agreement of the other person for that connection to click into place, though it's not a conscious agreement.

In a flash, their body-mind often agrees to respond to the feeling you are radiating before they can even process what has happened. It's all happening unconsciously, but that doesn't lessen its powerful effect.

Of course, there will always be times when it's appropriate to be private, and it's a wise idea to be selective about verbal disclosure. Generally, however, to be happy, to be fulfilled, be physically wide-open, vulnerable, and transparent.

Living for appearances weakens a person. Live for what is real in you. This helps you prove to yourself that you are someone of value. You are here on purpose, and for a purpose.

This week, be ultra-transparent, especially to yourself. Write about things you notice in the reactions from others, as well as your own personal growth.

Week Five: Energize your Cells

Use body awareness to infuse your cells with tingling energy. All it takes to feel the tingle of awakening cells is to focus on the feeling in different areas of your body.

Feel your fingers, toes, or any other part of your body to start. Scan your body from head to toe, front and back, your whole body from all sides again and again.

Over time, the tingling body awareness feelings will increase. Much like recovering from nerve damage, you will awaken nerve responses throughout your body with this practice.

Tuning into body awareness makes you ultra-sensitive. This energy sensation flows into your daily life, and positive changes begin right away.

There is a practice called, Yoga Nidra. Research this further for more help putting this into practice. It helps to have a sand timer. Watch the sand run out quietly as you keep your focus on one area or another of your body for at least two minutes.

Notice your own body position, the feeling in your hands, right hand, left hand, fingers, space between your fingers, right foot, left foot, toes and space between your toes, upper arms, lower calves and so on until you can feel your whole body pulsating with energy.

Next, you can feel the things around you, such as the breeze, subtle air pressure, your clothing, your breath through your nose and mouth, the air around your body and face.

Notice the warmth of sunlight through a window, the sounds of wind and water. Tune in to sounds near and then far. Notice where your body is in relation to objects such as the sofa, floor, and other ordinary things.

In addition to quiet meditation, movement, such as a physical practice like dance and yoga, will stimulate fluids even within your bones. This practice will energize your cells.

Yoga is a favorite because you can do it with just enough space for a mat, and your computer will have an abundance of classes in the privacy of your home.

According to Yoga Journal, "Synovial fluid is the slippery fluid that fills most of the body's joints allowing them to glide over each other without friction. This clear, slightly viscous fluid is also important because it delivers nutrients and oxygen to the hyaline cartilage, which—unlike most body tissues—doesn't have its own blood supply. Any joint movement helps circulate the synovial fluid, which feeds the cartilage; practicing yoga poses, therefore, helps keep the cartilage well-nourished."

After practice, write about what changes you or others seemed to notice.

Week Six: What You Can't See

Your brain can't notice everything, so it's selective and usually chooses to be aware of what it already knows.

Beware of the familiar, your habitual patterns, and what holds you to your comfort zone. These are things that sit well with your brain, but they hold you back when it comes to knowing your true nature.

According to Quanta Magazine, "Attentional processes are the brain's way of shining a searchlight on relevant stimuli and filtering out the rest."

That's understandable, there is often too much going on. Too much stimulation, too much information, even in the tiniest of interactions in every second as we go through our lives.

Being aware of it all would be overwhelming!

You can, however, start by *stretching* awareness. It will bring light to previously unused spaces within you. You will become more yourself, uncover more of yourself, and discover treasures inside you that are of extreme and precious value.

It's a lot like a fairly common dream many people have. Have you ever found new, undiscovered rooms and valuable items such as antique furniture in your dreams? I have. The exploration seems endless. The glorious feeling goes on and on until you awaken.

When you think about it, these dreams are reminders that there is more to life than you can see, more to *you* than you can see. You can't see it all, isn't that wonderful!

For centuries, people have made up "facts" when they want to feel like they already know everything. Some people think it's important to know everything. Do you agree there are some things best left unknown?

"There be dragons." I heard an example of this with the early explorers. When they created maps of the African Continent, they didn't know how to make a map for the areas farther north, so they just recorded, "Here lie dragons."

When we hear something discordant with our point of view, we make things up to protect ourselves. If it's outside of our comfort zone, we may feel cognitive dissonance, a strange sense of discomfort, so we may just shut it down or tune it out.

Instead, stay with this newness. If you are confined within what you already know, how can you improve your life? But, to avoid sensory overload, we have to stretch ourselves in tiny increments.

As you live with deliberate direction, you go off autopilot. Doing the same thing over and over is drudgery and it gets us nowhere. It's a treadmill.

Though it isn't always easy, it is worth the trouble to go *off autopilot.* Even if it's uncomfortable at first, it will make a difference in your life to be part of that which "holds the wheel."

When you decide to turn off habitual routine and tune in to life, in this moment, you are now here, rather than nowhere. If I can take a stab at quoting your GPS, "You have arrived."

Is there some part of reality that you're ignoring? Maybe it was always there, but you've tuned it out? What new thing are you just now noticing? Anything new, no matter how seemingly insignificant, make a note of it.

Week Seven: Everything as Funny

To increase your levity and attractive lighthearted nature, practice seeing everything as funny. The closest thing to being what you really are is to be relaxed, playful, and sometimes funny. To *be* funny, *see* funny.

Not everyone is funny, but everyone can see things from a slightly more humorous perspective. This relieves the stress of being a serious grownup, which is highly overrated.

There is even a meditation called, "Laughing Meditation." I prefer to find things that make me laugh more organically, but I have tried this meditation. It helps to loosen up the "laugh mechanism." Laughter then flows more easily. It's more of a way to get unstuck from feeling overly serious about life. Give your laugh muscle a tune-up, and laughter will flow more easily.

Go with it, whatever makes you laugh, no need to apologize. If it might be funny, just say it. There's one thing I've noticed about people that are funny, and that is they put themselves out there. You might get a laugh, or it could be just a courtesy snicker, but if you're going to be funny, you're going to have to test the water.

Every now and then, maybe too often, you're going to say something stupid or embarrassing. People usually just roll their eyes and forget about that, but they notice if you make them laugh.

A healthy humorous slant helps keep the mood light and easy. Most people have a great deal of respect for those who can make them laugh. Humor is another superpower, but it's not always easy. "Dying is easy, comedy is hard."

Notice everything during this week that could even possibly be seen as funny. Put your antennae out there for the absurd, life is, after all, quite peculiar. If you can, be funny. If that isn't natural for you, just notice what makes you laugh.

The world is so much brighter when it's twisted into something funny, so make that your focus this week, and write about your successes. You will definitely end up with some fun stories to tell. You may even end up with a new comedy set.

Week Eight: Interrupting - It's Annoying

Nothing puts a screeching halt to the positive energy of a conversation more quickly than interrupting. It's a huge letdown, "You weren't really listening? You were just waiting to talk!"

Most of us have a terrible time slowing down enough to really listen. Listening without interrupting, or without thinking about what you're going to say, is imperative, but it's often a challenge. Let's take a look at what might be happening:

Paying attention is relative. I remember my beautiful second-grade teacher. I paid attention to her because she was so kind, but I rarely heard what she was saying.

She would bend down closely and talk with me, smiling while explaining to me a work page.

I don't remember comprehending much of what she said. I paid attention to all the wrong things; her eyes, her smile, and her mouth moving as she spoke. I couldn't seem to hear what she was saying, because I was concentrating on what was naturally attracting my attention.

This is the way we are built to respond. As children, we are drawn into that which has the most positive energy. As adults, this is also true, but we benefit from paying attention to content as well.

Content may not have positive energy flowing through it, but if we learn how to listen, we'll get more of the plot in the interaction, and in life itself.

When you leave, even for a few seconds in the middle of a movie, you often lose a big part of the plot. It takes a while to catch up if you even can. When we learn how to listen, even when it's boring, we'll get a better grasp of what's going on. If we don't, we risk losing the plot and looking like an idiot.

Listening is probably the hardest part of communication. We pay attention to the mood or feeling in the room, our own thoughts, the inner or outer beauty of a person, the brightness of colors, or anything that's moving. All of this holds our attention much more easily than words. We all have some level of distractibility, especially when we're listening to words.

We can become impatient. We may feel like we already know where the speaker is going, and we decide to finish their sentence for them.

Perhaps they're talking too long, or their topic isn't in your wheelhouse. You might be worried that you have something great to say, and if you don't interrupt, you're going to forget your reply, on it goes.

How do you feel when the situation is reversed? Are you annoyed when you're interrupted? Do you feel dismissed? Did the other person really know what you were going to say? Was their point so life-changing that it warranted blowing you off and derailing your train of thought?

Most likely you allow people to interrupt you, and they allow you to interrupt them, but it's a big issue.

What comes to your mind when someone is talking? Are they boring? Does it remind you of the time when you (fill in the blank)?

You may also realize that if you let someone go on and on without interrupting, they don't seem to know when to stop. Just please, find a place to put a period already!

In our busy lives, being interrupted is commonplace. Sometimes we're interrupted not with words, but with cell phones. A friend has to take a call or check a post on social media while you, sitting right in front of them, get ignored. Have you done this? I have, but it's not polite. It can leave you feeling like you don't matter.

Fred Rogers wrote, "Listening is where love begins; listening to ourselves and then our neighbors." It seems that Mister Rogers never left people feeling unimportant.

When you get excited and start to interrupt, take a breath, and stop yourself. Think about how you're making them feel. Be honest about what's making you want to interrupt or half-listen.

What do you notice about interrupting as you go through this week? Does listening get easier over time? Do people feel more engaged with you when you listen? How is this practice changing your relationships?

Week Nine: Good Vibrations

At a private school, I worked with a child who had special needs. He was especially present. It could be partly due to his natural quietness, but he had beautiful, palpable energy. He did not have a busy mind, and this contributed to his good vibrations.

This young man had a simple way of being that was purely magnetic. Everyone felt it. They also felt free to comment on this loving energy. He glowed with "feeling." Usually people don't say anything when they notice the feeling someone has, but in his case, perhaps because of his special need, people felt free to tell him how impressed they were by his good vibrations.

You don't have to be young, good-looking, or even immensely positive to have good vibrations. All you really need is a quiet mind, an aware body, a general appreciation for others, and highly focused, but soft, attention.

Practice things that bring you closer to these attributes, and you will have irresistibly good vibrations.

One practice is an actual vibration. Put your hands on your chest and say, "ohm." Feel that sensation. In some eastern religions it is said that the universe, and all things were created with this sound.

This practice comes from the East, but you don't have to believe in that, or anything specific like that, to increase good vibrations.

Vibrations are known throughout the world in one form or another. Whether it's the vibration of ohm, words spoken in sacred texts, or vibration in the scientific idea of "String theory" as an example, vibrations matter.

If you're not familiar with string theory, PBS's Nova states, "According to string theory, absolutely everything in the universe—all of the particles that make up matter and forces—is comprised of tiny vibrating fundamental strings.")

Also consider the biblical idea of "The Word." John: 1:1 "In the beginning was the Word, and the Word was *with* God and the Word *was* God."

Doesn't it all have a similar "ring" to it? All these sacred religious and scientific ideas appear to be talking about the reality and the importance of vibrations. How beautiful is it that creation is more like music than a bunch of physical things?

A sound such as a singing bowl, a bell, sacred music, fun music, whatever floats your vibration upwards, practice that.

There are vibrations going on all around us. Some are too fast and some are too slow to detect with our senses. The low rumble of a truck passing by, and the high sound of a bat using echolocation, these are both beyond the abilities of our senses.

While there are worlds beyond and outside of your senses, tune into a sound or vibration that is barely perceptible. Listen to the sound of a low voice, or song with a high pitch. Stretch your ability to feel and hear vibrations.

Another practice would be to use sound and mix it with body awareness. When one sense crosses over into another it's called synesthesia. For example, it might be that you taste color or feel sound.

Applying this to increasing your sense of vibration, try this experiment: Listen to a flowing stream and imagine the sound is flowing in your hands. Do your hands tingle? Also, try putting music you enjoy into the sensations in your feet or another part of your body. "Feeling the beat" helps with your sense of rhythm and flow.

Rhythmic sound synchronizes brainwaves and has other more subtle advantages.

This week, tune into good vibrations. Increase the space in your brain for vibration sensation. Vibrate your feelings upward, feel better and better vibrationally, then write about what new, good things you notice.

Week Ten: An Upward Trend

Things are supposed to spiral down if left unchecked. This is the nature and simple science of entropy. You cannot coast. You either go up or you go down.

If you are to spiral upwards, however, you're going to have to work at it. Apply a practice that leads to an upward trend, against the law of entropy.

Since the second law of thermodynamics states that, left unattended, all things trend toward disorder, this week's challenge is to attend to the disorder. Move disorder intentionally towards order.

The laws of entropy are challenged by an increase in life's complexity. There is an upward trend towards intelligent and complex life. This suggests that some kind of force is tending to life. Tune into this life force.

If only survival mattered, no earthly creature would have had to develop beyond a simple organism.

More than survival matters to you. You are looking for meditations that empower you. Drive your life upwards towards beauty and order. Get in alignment with this upward trend. Feel the wonder of the underlying force that moves you towards improvement.

If the craters on the moon are a result of the cosmic chaos of creation, banging into each other, what if we are still banging into each other when we fight?

Fighting is a kind of chaotic disorder. If you are to move upwards, you'll want to learn to get curious rather than getting into a fight. See what you can learn about yourself that makes you mad. I never trust getting angry too often, it leads to chaos. Cool off before continuing any kind of heated exchange.

Over time the planets cool, they find their orbit. Can you find your orbit in all that is chaos?

Take any area of chaos in your life and move it towards order. Everything that needs organizing, thoughts, your room, your relationships, the things you believe in, they should all move up from chaos to order.

There is peace in order. We either snowball up into greater order or down into chaos. How do you fall up?

By being part of that underlying force of nature that cares.

Work against the entropy, laziness, and disorder that shows up in any form, disrupting your life. When Harrison Ford was asked during an interview about "The Force," he said, "Force Yourself."

This week, write about creating order out of chaos. Trend Upwards.

Week Eleven:
Enhancing Your Romantic Lens

Your romantic lens packs in much more than a simple "lover" relationship, though it definitely helps with that too. Overall, however, it is more about falling in love with life itself.

There are many ways to view the world. Your worldview is supple, flexible, and transformable. Romance is a realistic way in which to view everything around you, and it is a Golden Key. Use it to open to a world of romantic adventure.

When we are bombarded with fear tactics from the media, bad news about good people we admire, and other black and cloudy lenses, we are wounded. We can undo this damage to our perspective by re-looking *at it all* through a romantic lens.

This is a "correction" more than a false viewpoint. This is how you saw things when you were a child, long before you were corrupted by the agenda of the Adult World.

The draw of a romantic practice increases in you a magnetic radiation of energy. It attracts more beauty, delight, and fulfillment to you, and *in* you.

If you want to feel romantic about life, practice it. Little by little you will see the reality of it when you do. Life is romantic.

These dimensions of romantic reality don't open up to you easily. They have to be gently and persistently persuaded to appear. If you don't embrace the romantic dimensions, they are like a shy, untouched door, a forever unopened door. Never opened, never seen, never known as real.

Romanticize, and know this reality. While your soft gaze is focused into the eyes of another, listen, see, and feel their heart and mind. Notice everything beautiful, like the dazzled eyes of one beholding another in love.

Look with wonder at the wind in the trees, the quietness of clouds, and the spark of mischief in the eyes of another. There is a teasing draw from your reality, it's asking you to move in closer, with a softer perspective, towards the warmth of a romantic view.

You can even see the sadness in the world differently, more clearly, through a romantic lens. Look at everything as if it had a powerful purpose. You can even superimpose a sense of beautiful background music. Because everything really is romantic, and everything *does* have a powerful meaning.

Week Twelve: Sending Sensations

Play a game with a friend, someone who is easygoing and naturally centered physically would be helpful.

While blindfolded with your back turned to your partner, ask them to stand several feet away. Then, as they sneak up behind you, see if they can send energy strong enough for you to feel it. It helps to put energy into the hands, as if they were lightsabers or as if your fingers glowed with streaming light.

Take turns with the exercise and notice what you can sense. See if you can feel your friend approaching. When you think they're within arm's reach, turn around quickly to see where they're standing. Were you right?

In the same way that micro-expressions give away feelings, there are micro-sounds and changes in air pressure that help give away the location of the person sneaking up on you.

If you get better at sensing this, you'll become a super-sensor. If you get better at sending this feeling out from your body-mind, you'll become a super-sender.

When you can sense sensations coming at you, you'll get better at sending sensations outwards from your body as well.

Another practice in sending sensations is to stop before you reach something, then continue on as usual.

This is so powerful, it's used by some police officers. As you go through your day, stop every now and then and send energy towards ordinary things.

When you make a sandwich, stop, grab it, then take a bite. When you're cleaning with a vacuum, stop, reach for the handle, then continue.

Sending energy out before you reach for something is done in martial arts. That I know because I was a martial arts instructor for many years. What surprised me, however, was that a police officer said this practice keeps him from making grave mistakes. Before he grabs his gun, he stops, then continues reaching for his gun. This ensures his aim will be better, and so will his judgment, before taking action against a suspect.

What else can you sense behind and around you or outside of your visual and peripheral perception? Can others feel you sending energy? Write about what you discover.

Week Thirteen: Radiating the Light of Presence

Presence is pure power. It's felt beyond the body and is sent out to the people, and all the creatures, around you if they will listen. Like a dog that can smell love or fear, your presence has an aroma. It's sending out constant information about what you're feeling. If that's received, heard, and understood, you then have the power to influence others to feel better along with you.

Goodness and openness, combined with presence, brings peace, not only to you, but to anyone who comes in contact with you. You have your background of learning what *not to do,* we all need that before deciding to be, what we consider, "good." Once you are where you believe you should be, you'll radiate that confidence in yourself out to others.

People appreciate the light of presence obvious in someone who is "fully here." You are there for them when you radiate silent presence. People respond to this on some primal level, even if they don't know what or why they're responding. Draw others in with your presence and they will want to be around it whenever possible.

Part of presence is just being here fully in the moment, as well as being there for other people when they need you. Of course, there is more to it than that.

When you speak, move, and live with all of the attributes previously mentioned, and you practice those attributes, you will cultivate a presence of immeasurable worth.

Another part of presence is pure awareness of others, without any baggage between you. To tune into someone else's pure presence, try to sense the essence emanating from them or "the feeling" they have.

It's common knowledge that people have a presence, and that it lingers. Like a room that is thick with tension after an argument or contagious laughter leaves joy that stays in the walls, you can sense the feeling emanating in others. It's something beyond the body and beyond time.

You have a feeling that emanates from you; everyone and everything does. Increase this "feeling" and you'll increase your presence. You will also increase the ability to feel the presence of another.

Everyone knows what presence is, and everyone wants more of it. We all know when someone has or doesn't have presence, but what is it? How can you really make it grow? All the practices in this book will help. You will find more of your own ways to cultivate it too. It's fun when you see people respond to changes in your presence without knowing why. You begin to feel them feel you.

It feels empowering when others feel your presence power. When they feel you, it increases that feeling within you and between you. Your wavelengths begin to match up and the presence in you and another continues to intensify, like a laser beam.

According to Nasa,
"Lasers produce a narrow beam of light in which all of the light waves have very similar wavelengths. The laser's light waves travel together with their peaks all lined up, or in phase. This is why laser beams are very narrow, very bright, and can be focused into a very tiny spot."

Presence is so subtle, many people can't articulate why they like it or what it is, but presence is felt and recognized as captivating and irresistible.

When you are fully aware, the light of your presence reveals your inner power and it changes things for the better. Your sense of passion and intensity, your awareness and spirit, people get caught up in it. It's a miraculous interweaving of body and soul. This feeling is an empowering source of strength.

In each interaction, whoever's presence is stronger has greater influence. Usually, if only by default, it's the negative emotions that are more influential. They are often stronger than positive ones because of our negativity bias.

It's natural to be more tuned into the negative because you have to deal with threats, but you don't *have to* deal with positive and beautiful things.

If you're walking between two bushes, one with a snake that bites, and one with beautiful flowers, which bush do you keep your attention on? The one with the snake. You can't ignore a threat without consequences. This is why there is a negativity bias.

Because negativity can be so influential, your positive presence has to be honed and practiced. When you do this through discipline, you increase your power to help yourself, and others, to overcome our negativity bias.

Do you hope to help people feel inspired along with you? The root meaning of the word "inspire" has to do with breathing life into something. Presence is breathing some unspeakable something in, then sending it out into others.

Cultivate presence energy, then write about your observations.

Week Fifteen: Unghost Yourself

Do you want to be seen and heard? Then, in a word, summarize. This week create a haiku. A haiku is a poem that uses only seventeen syllables. Five syllables on the first line, seven on the second, and then five on the last line.

Though they used to be mainly poems about nature, your haiku can be about anything that matters to you. You can start by writing about whatever comes to mind, don't shorten it or censor yourself, just write freely.

Take that big idea and circle your best points. Then write anything that feels important to you or that moves you. Find the words that feel beautiful, poignant, or funny. Finally, condense it all down to 17 syllables.

Writing these poems is a practice in condensing our thoughts and eliminating unnecessary words.

This is what it takes for others to really see and hear you. Big ideas, or simple ideas, but whatever your ideas, express them in as few words as possible.

Feeling Like a Ghost?
Magically Appear Again
Encapsulate Thoughts

Now that you are heard, you will be seen, both inside and out. When you speak, say something of value, something that increases honesty, a sense of humor, or the joy of being alive. You are now unghosted.

When you are seen because others can now really afford the energy to listen deeply, they will begin to see through to your sweet, natural beauty.

Knowing people are likely seeing right through *to you* and not just *through you*, you will be inspired to further your inner development.

Find things within that you want to clean up more thoroughly. You'll want to make your insides even more beautiful and presentable for those who can deeply perceive you.

Considering that you might be really "seen" deeply by others, and in a powerfully primal way, what would you change? When you feel like you're seeing into others, what do you notice? Do you think it's a real thing to see through to others? What do you feel inside when others can really see you?

Week Sixteen: Delicious Body Awareness

Awareness is golden, silent, and healing. There is more to it than just a function of the brain. I first noticed this years ago during an extremely difficult time. I didn't have faith in anything, and without faith in life, I struggled with fear and insomnia.

One night, while having trouble falling asleep, I began to focus on the feeling of the bottoms of my feet. I felt instantly grounded as the stream of thought and worry came to an abrupt stop.

Each time I felt my feet or any other part of my body, I felt relieved. It was like I had been falling, but now I touched solid ground, where everything was good again.

When you can find a way to get past your troubled mind through your body, it is a healing awareness. Living in a state of healed awareness brings peace. Without peace, there is no joy or even love, anxiety overwhelms and drowns out these other, more subtle emotions.

Earlier I mentioned, Yoga Nidra. There is also the practice of Gestalt. One from the East and the other from the West, these forms of body awareness are healing, revealing, and relaxing.

You can up your game by feeling emotions in your body. No matter what culture or religion you prefer, just stay with your emotions, know where they are in your body, and then write about what happens.

Week Seventeen: Mirroring as an A.R.T.

Let's focus first on emotional mirroring. This is when you repeat back what someone said to you. This shows them that you are listening and that you understand their point.

Practice sessions of mirroring with a friend will reveal how good you really are at this. We often don't realize how much we assume, and we lose huge segments of information because of it.

Mirroring can be done emotionally, but it can also be done physically. Again, the physical has an effect on the emotional connection as well. Now, put this into practice with a partner.

Start by standing face-to-face with your partner. Put your palms facing their palms and move your hands and arms in unison as if your partner is a mirror image.

Play peaceful music or nature sounds in the background. See if you can move like flowing water together, a meditation without tension, as you become one with the other person.

We used mirroring to avoid punches in martial arts. Just imagine your body moving naturally like a mirror as a fist is thrown at you. With practice, you can move gracefully out of the way, like a dancer. As the boxer, Muhammad Ali said, "float like a butterfly." But in this exercise, we won't sting like a bee.

You can use this practice for increased sensitivity to others. What's the advantage of sensitivity? If they can feel you, they become one with you. They become invested in your well-being, interested in going further into the relationship with you, and they are less likely to want to hurt you emotionally or physically.

According to an article by Psychiatry and Psychotherapy, there was a discovery in 1992. While looking at monkeys' brains with electrodes, researchers accidentally discovered that the same neurons were activated in the monkey's brain whether the monkey picked up a piece of fruit or the monkey just watched the researcher picking up a piece of fruit. That same team published a paper that showed these mirror neurons respond to mouth actions and facial expressions.

This is important information because when you move with another, even subtly through facial expression, you can activate their mirror neurons and sync up with them emotionally. This increases empathy and empathy makes *causing* good feelings enjoyable. It also makes *causing* any kind of harmful feelings uncomfortable.

Connect with yourself at the end of a mirroring session. Set a three-minute timer (longer if you prefer) then state out loud what you see, hear, or feel. If you feel your heartbeat, say "heart," if you're thinking, say "thought." The idea is to float with your mind, wherever it wants to go.

To look further into this, read about Vipassana meditations, one of India's most ancient forms of healing.

When you want to interact with someone effectively, there is an art to listening. It's a lot like the mirroring practice.

The A.R.T. of Mirroring

A. Ask for and give feedback. "How' am I doing? Am I understanding you correctly?"

R. Ratio of 6 to 1. "Here are my concerns as well as some positive observations." Consider using a popular ratio of six specific, positive compliments for each constructive suggestion.

T. Turn it around. Rather than the usual, compliment first, put the compliment last. Turn the order around. We usually compliment first, then make our suggestion. "You are a good friend, but you're always late." Now feel how it sounds when you say, "You're always late, but you are a good friend."

After your experience with these kinds of mirroring practices, write about any change you may notice, especially a change in energy or state of mind.

Week Eighteen: Your Hands Hold the Key

Have you ever noticed that people often meditate or pray with their palms up? When you do that, the sensation in your hands is expanded.

Why would you want to increase the sensation in your hands? Anywhere you increase sensation, you increase presence power, but hands are exceptionally important for conveying energy, communication, and self-awareness.

Hands have more sensory neurons that send information to your mind and body. The epidermal ridges on the surface of the fingertips help us to feel pressure, heat, and texture.

The tingling sensation in your hands increases awareness through meditation. One meditation is resting, palms up after clapping your hands.

Feet are also important for sensation. Isn't it a meditation just to take your shoes off in the grass or on the beach?

In yoga, practitioners spread their toes out to increase awareness there. I've done that for long enough now, that I can move my other toes more independently. My baby toe and middle toes definitely have more control and sensation than when I first started.

These kinds of awareness practices are useful for more than regaining sensation, they are useful in intensifying it.

After increasing sensation in my hands, I had an experience that validated this. Just before throwing a punch at a new dojo while practicing with a blue belt, he looked wide-eyed at my hands and said, "There's something powerful about your hands." I think awareness in your hands helps with hugs, handshakes, and intimacy.

Place your hands on your lap palms facing upwards. Squeeze the left and right hands alternately while you allow your mind to go wherever it chooses. Speak openly about whatever comes to mind and then write about it afterward.

Alternatively, you can lie down on the ground with palms facing up. Clap three times so that you can feel the tingling in your hands. Stay with this feeling, breathe through your hands, and watch what you notice as long as your mind is quiet.

Next, reach your fingers toward the ceiling. Imagine you can feel the ceiling in as much detail as possible. Wiggle your fingers and imagine you can touch the texture of the paint. Now imagine your fingers are elongated lights or like flashlights touching the ceiling. If awareness is affected, you'll feel tingling in your fingers. Keep this up until you feel the tips of your fingers and the spaces between your fingers all the time, naturally.

Chemistry

I'm sure you've noticed the shift in awareness when someone new joins a conversation, or when someone leaves. Adding or subtracting anyone to anything changes the chemistry. More people make the interaction interesting and complex, fewer people can make it more intimate.

When some people walk in a room, the mood lightens. Another person may disrupt or darken an otherwise good conversation. "If anybody needs me, I'll be on the corner of Loneliness and Nobody Loves Me."
~Debbie Downer

If you apply this to molecules, like water for example, one tiny change makes a big difference. Water (H_2O) is made of the same elements as hydrogen peroxide, but hydrogen peroxide (H2O2) has only one tiny molecule more. Just one slight change in relational interactions, and you feel a sense of being healed. Another walks in, and it feels like a cool glass of water, quenching your thirst. Each person changes the chemistry of a room.

What do you observe as you watch the chemistry between people in a group setting? Does it seem like some of what you're feeling can be felt? What do you notice about the feeling going back and forth between other people involved in the conversation?

Do you feel someone feeling you when you watch them? My husband and I saw a sleeping duck. She was standing up, but her beak was tucked under her wing. We drove by, and then he backed up to show me. We thought she was cute so we watched her for a minute, when I said, "Do you think she can feel us watching her?" I intensified my gaze, and the duck turned to look at us. It could have been a coincidence, but the timing was perfect.

While interacting, notice what feels positive or negative. Watch moods dance, ebb, and flow. Can you feel a person change your mood? Does it also change your brain chemistry? Write about what you think.

What You Believe Matters

Things like rituals, diet, prayer, meditation, exercise, awareness of nature and your body, etc., these practices can mean the difference between being seriously ill and living a healthy, full life.

A study on the Mayo Clinic website confirms that what you believe matters, "A majority of the nearly 350 studies of physical health and 850 studies of mental health that have used religious and spiritual variables have found that religious involvement and spirituality are associated with better health outcomes." Regarding mortality, the Mayo clinic stated, "During the past 3 decades, at least 18 prospective studies have shown that religiously involved persons live longer. The populations examined in these studies include not only entire communities but also specific groups."

So, if what you believe matters, if it isn't practiced, then is it really what you believe? It can be, but if you want to move mountains, put it into practice. While we are incredibly impulsive, and we know what we should be doing, make it what you *could* be doing. Make that a habit and watch the changes you create in your life.

We may believe in something, but still feel the tug of an addiction. It might be the call of sugar or it might be something worse. It takes discipline to counteract discomfort.

Small changes make a big difference. Even if you don't want to give up all your vices, you could gain traction by toning down bad habits, and ramping up better ones, moving toward one good thing at a time. We learn in increments. If you stretch a rubber band too far too fast, it will snap. Ease into living what you believe, one choice at a time.

Whatever bad habits you may struggle with, it's not necessary to get down on yourself, there's no way to be perfect. Just noticing bad habits can be enough to change them naturally.

Awareness is a mystery. The reality of this was clarified for me after I injured my ankle. Weeks had passed, and it wasn't going to get better. I finally went to a physical therapist. "Stand on your foot and roll your ankle around. Just feel it, and your body will learn how to go around the pain," he advised. I was astonished that, after all that time, all that pain and weakness, and this simple exercise did the trick.

No need for surgery or special exercises, just feeling for and avoiding the pain, and my ankle is healed? Is it really that easy? It was in this case anyway. It's another tool to use for mild injuries, addictions, and bad decisions.

Sometimes you feel it to heal it. Write about anything you've found in the way of healing through awareness.

Believe in Yourself

I asked a group I run on social media how they prepare the people they love for real life. The answers I got were all about self-confidence, believing in yourself, and believing in something bigger than yourself.

Believing in more than yourself is one of the main objectives in Twelve Step programs. You can believe in whatever you like, they don't make you accept a certain religion, but they do say you have to have faith in something with more power than you have on your own.

To believe in yourself has many definitions. For some, it means that you feel good enough. Others might feel you just have to be a decent person. Collins Dictionary defines it as "confidence in oneself and one's abilities". Wiki How says to believe in yourself you must do three things: "nurture positive views, talk to people who love you, and find a cause that you believe in."

Jack Canfield, author of the series Chicken Soup for the Soul states, "In order to believe in yourself, you first have to believe that what you want is possible. Scientists used to believe that humans responded to information flowing into the brain from the outside world. But what we now know is that instead, we respond to what the brain, based on previous experience, expects to happen next."

Do you expect positive things? Seeing the positive in a world that appears to be difficult like ours; this takes muscles, awareness practices, and persistence.

There is one way that *doesn't* help you to believe in yourself, and that is to feel like a victim. The victim in any scenario attracts attention, "Are you okay? Poor baby." And that is it, that's all you get.

If you get better, and you are okay, you are no longer attracting people who feel sorry for you. What good is that anyway? Victims don't get better. All a victim gets is a pat on the back, words of affirmation, sympathy, and advice. They don't get healing, not when they're waiting on other people to rescue them. Do reach out, but not as a victim.

We can help each other, for sure, and we should, but get out of the victim mentality as soon as you see it. It won't serve you well in the long run.

In order to believe in yourself, you'll want to believe that you are competent. If you're not, then you'll want to train yourself to be. Your competency has to be real in *your eyes*, not anyone else's.

Get to a place where *you* respect your efforts. Do whatever it takes. If you don't believe in yourself, all the compliments, pats on the back, and trophies in the world won't help. *You* have to respect you.

When you feel like an imposter, you can't take the encouragement others give you to heart. Studies show that you have to feel like *you* earned it.

A good example of the strength that comes from trust in the other's abilities was on the playground. When my kids were little, I found they learned best when almost left alone. I was there close by, but I neither hovered nor ignored them. I noticed that the parents who were less worried about their kids, had stronger children. Some of the strongest kids were the ones that were neglected, if they survived.

The parents who hovered, warning and worrying, had worried kids who couldn't do as much without falling.

It seemed best to be close by in case things got serious, but we let the kids fall, at least a little before catching them. That way they get a feel for, and better understand balance. Let yourself and others feel their loss of balance whenever it is reasonably safe.

In one case our kids were all having a good time together on the swings. A friend's five-year-old boy was swinging with us without a problem for quite some time when his mother came running out shouting, "He can't swing, he doesn't know how!" Believing his mom, the kid opened both his hands and let go. He fell to the ground crying.

Don't let go of your practices. Hold to them and know you can do it! Combining realism with a positive perspective and intention works to make you someone *you* can believe in.

Step it up to the next realistic, but more enjoyable perspective. Move in increments towards all the amazing things you can become. Step up to the role of the hero. You are your own hero.

Do whatever it takes *not* to be a victim of negativity. Write about your heroic adventures in positive presence power. Paint that picture with some creative finesse to bring what you want even closer.

There is more purpose to your life than can be discovered with just your senses alone. Through your senses, however, not instead of them, you take yourself to higher ground.

It's your story, make it matter, make it funny, romantic, ever better, and you will make it through to your true, relaxed nature.

I hope this information about the softness of Ki and Inner Aikido translates well through these words. It would be so much easier to show you face-to-face. I will set up YouTubes in the future under Innerlightlearning.com. I sincerely hope it helps you understand the Power of Softness even better than before.

I want to be of service, and don't know if my writing can help, but it's the most prolific way to reach out to others and share what I've learned through these life practices. Softness makes the lessons in life more tolerable. More gets through to you, and more internal strength shows up when times change, and become more difficult.

If you enjoyed this book and find you were able to move forward using some of its principles, please leave a review and I will also make this book an audible. Through voice, I can send Ki, filling it with "the feeling" so it flows to you. This could help give you a good night's sleep, a powerful start to your day. May you live your life with The Power of Softness. Thank you, and may you be Blessed.

~Alethea C. Sensei